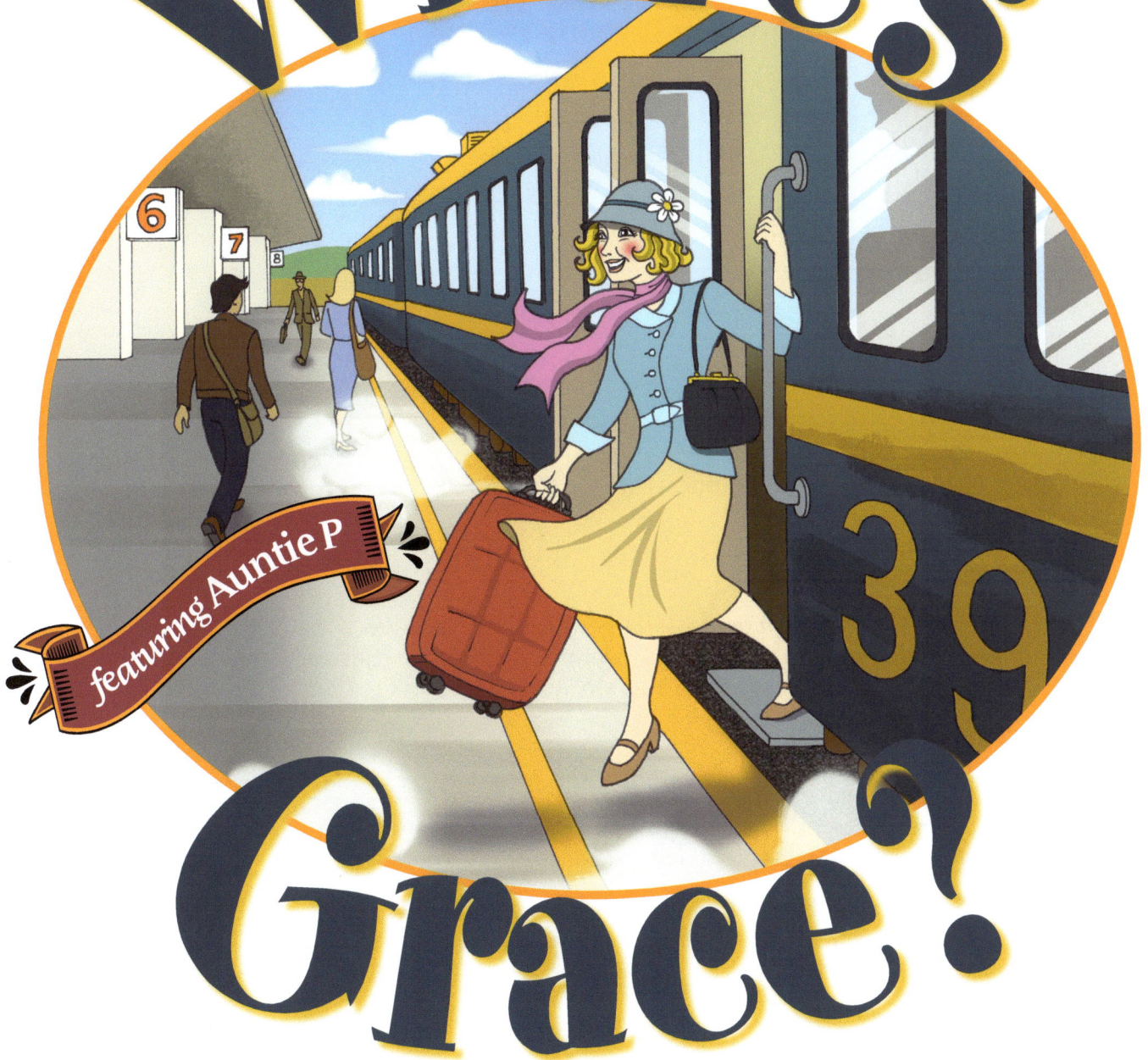

Where's Grace?

featuring Auntie P

by Patricia Kearney

Illustrations by Dexter Santos

*"As you walk the roads, may you always
have a kind word for those you meet."*

TRADITIONAL IRISH/ADAPTED BY PHIL COULTER

DEDICATION

This book is dedicated to all the young girls and
boys seeking to be more than commonplace
and hoping to walk (and hopefully also "dance")
through life with style, intelligence and grace.
You know who you are. May you always find grace
and live in its beauty, the best way you can.
When you find it, pass it on.

Connolly, Hayes & Heffernan Publishers
P. O. Box 40322
Pittsburgh, PA 15201
www.auntiep.com

Second Printing, March 1, 2013
ISBN: 978-0-615-48563-8
Library of Congress Cataloging-in-Publication Data
Library of Congress Control Number: 2011912891
Where's Grace? \Kearney-McCarty, Patricia

The paper used in this publication meets the minimum requirements of the
American National Standards for Information Sciences—Permanence of Paper
for the Printed Library Materials ANSI Z39.48-1992.

Special thanks to Elizabeth, Robby and Christian Flory for their wonderful
inspiration and grace in all they do each day, and thank you to Girard Tournesol,
Patricia Thrushart, Soo Clark, Ernst, Carolann Cioffi DeSantis, and Frank Andrews.

Illustrations: Dexter Santos
Design: Paulette Green, P Green Design
Back Cover Photo: Michele D'Emo

Elizabeth's Auntie Patricia

usually visits Elizabeth's family every few months. She arrives by train with her small bag and dancing shoes. Elizabeth and her two brothers, Robby and Chris, look forward to Auntie P's visits, knowing that she will tell them about her recent travels and about her love for Duke Ellington music.

The children yell, "Hi, Auntie P!" They greet her, giving kisses and hugs as if she had been away forever! Elizabeth loves calling her Aunt Patricia Auntie P. It makes her giggle inside.

That night at dinner everyone is gathered around the table enjoying the wonderful meal Elizabeth's Mother had cooked. Elizabeth and her brothers helped to set the table.

Everyone always has their chores, putting dishes, glasses, napkins and silverware on the table for the evening meal. Elizabeth's Father also cuts flowers from the garden in honor of Auntie P's visit.

Auntie P talks with great joy about her love for Swing music and music of the 20's, 30's and 40's. Everyone always enjoys stories about her visits to the Catalina Island's Swing Dance Festival in California.

Auntie P says, "Oh, it was so wonderful, seeing all the people dancing on the beautiful ballroom floor at the Avalon Ballroom by the water. The nights were filled with fun, laughter and the music of Duke Ellington! Duke Ellington had style and elegance. He was so full of grace."

"I wish people had that kind of grace today," says Auntie P. "People are always yelling at each other on TV and in the street these days ... no grace at all. I wish people would remember what a little grace could do to make things better in the world."

The next day, Elizabeth tells her best friend Barry that her Aunt Patricia has come in from the city for a short visit with the family and that during dinner Auntie P talked about her favorite music—music from the 1920's, 1930's and 1940's.

"Auntie P told us how much fun the Swing Dance Festival in Catalina was and how everyone enjoys the music and dances every dance," says Elizabeth. "Auntie P also talked about how no one has grace anymore," exclaims Elizabeth. "She said that people used to be kind and had more grace, now all you hear and see on TV are people yelling and being rude to each other."

AMAZING GRACE...

Elizabeth asks Barry, "I wonder if we could get some? It seems like it's very important to have grace. Where do you think we could find it? Do you know what it is and where we could get it?"

Barry tells Elizabeth that he remembers in church that someone said that grace was "amazing."

While walking down the block, Barry and Elizabeth see their friend Leila on the steps opening a box. Elizabeth asks Leila, "Have you heard about grace at all?"

Leila shows Barry and Elizabeth her new shoes. "Well, I just got some new shoes in the color *pink grace* and they are now my very favorites," says Leila. Elizabeth tells Leila, "I don't think that's what grace is all about."

"But they're pink," says Leila. Barry asks Leila, "What about the amazing part?" Leila shows Barry, "They have a **bow. ...**"

Elizabeth remarks, "You know before dinner my Dad said grace and everyone bowed their heads and felt thankful for the meal my Mom made."

Barry comments, "Well, if that's it ... why did your Aunt say that no one has grace anymore?"

Elizabeth admits, "Yes, you are probably right. It's one thing to say it and another to have it I guess."

Elizabeth and Barry see their neighbor Grace through an open window of her house. Grace greets Barry and Elizabeth with a big hello, "Where are you going? Come on in."

Elizabeth tells Grace that they are trying to figure out how to find grace!

Grace overjoyed says, "Well, here I am!"

"I don't think Elizabeth's Auntie P means that
we should find a person named Grace," says Barry.
"I think she means we need to get some grace."

Elizabeth asks, "Can you tell us anything about
having grace?"

Grace tells Barry and Elizabeth, "I do try to think of others, but, well, I work all day trying to keep my head above water, expanding my home business. I'm on the computer and phone all day."

Grace says, "There's no time it seems to get all of my projects done and think of new ones, I mean think about other people. Oh, did you and Barry want something?" Grace appears very preoccupied.

"No, we were just talking. Nothing special," says Barry.

"It's OK," says Elizabeth. "We will be going now."
They bid goodbye to Grace. Elizabeth exclaims,
"Oh, it seems that grown-ups never have much
time!" Barry nods his head in agreement.

Elizabeth and Barry yell to a woman carrying
many packages and crossing the street, "Hey, there,
let us help!"

Their favorite crosswalk guard, Gina, comes running toward them. "That was a gracious thing for you both to do. ... very nice of you both," says Gina.

Barry tells Gina, "Oh, it's nothing. ... we just do that ... it's nothing. She needed some help."

Gina says, "Well, it was a very nice thing to do."

Barry and Elizabeth walk down the street and feel that they will never find the meaning of grace or having grace.

On their way back to Elizabeth's house, Elizabeth and Barry see their neighbor's kitten, Zayna, has climbed up a tree and that their neighbor Ka'Maul is calling for help to retrieve his little Persian cat.

Ka'Maul yells, "There she is ... little Zayna far up in the Oak tree. Oh, no," yells Ka'Maul. "No one will be able to get her down!"

Barry removes his glasses and climbs up the tree. When he reaches the branch where Zayna is perched, he reaches out easily to grasp her and brings her safely to the ground.

Ka'Maul is so thankful and says that Zayna is his only one beautiful cat in the whole world.

"Zayna means beauty you know," he tells Barry and Elizabeth. "Thank you so much," Ka'Maul says over and over.

Barry tells Ka'Maul that he was happy to be there when Ka'Maul and little Zayna needed him and that he would have felt bad if Ka'Maul would be unhappy all day.

At home Elizabeth greets Auntie P. "Where's grace Auntie P? It seems that I don't know what grace really is or how to get it. In my entire search, I'm more confused than ever."

"Oh, dear," said Auntie P. "You can change the world by the small things you do for others all the time. Grace is all about that. You don't need to be rich and famous or tall or thin to act considerate and show kindness toward others."

It doesn't cost a dime to say a kind word or hold out your hand to someone needing comfort.

Auntie P tells Elizabeth, "Even helping Mom with the dishes without her asking is a graceful act. Grace is even just helping someone out. Grace can be everywhere, in the everyday experiences you share.

"When you treat others with grace your friends will respond with kindness and be thankful. I'm sure you remember when someone was nice to you! Can you remember?"

"Yes," exclaims Elizabeth, "especially you Auntie P!"

"Well then children of grace," said Auntie P,
"I will share with you all how to dance the
Shim Sham! It's simple dimple!"

**Life is wonderful when you
share what you've learned.**

You can be sure that there's always something new.

"Okay kids, *Shim Sham*. ... Let's go!"

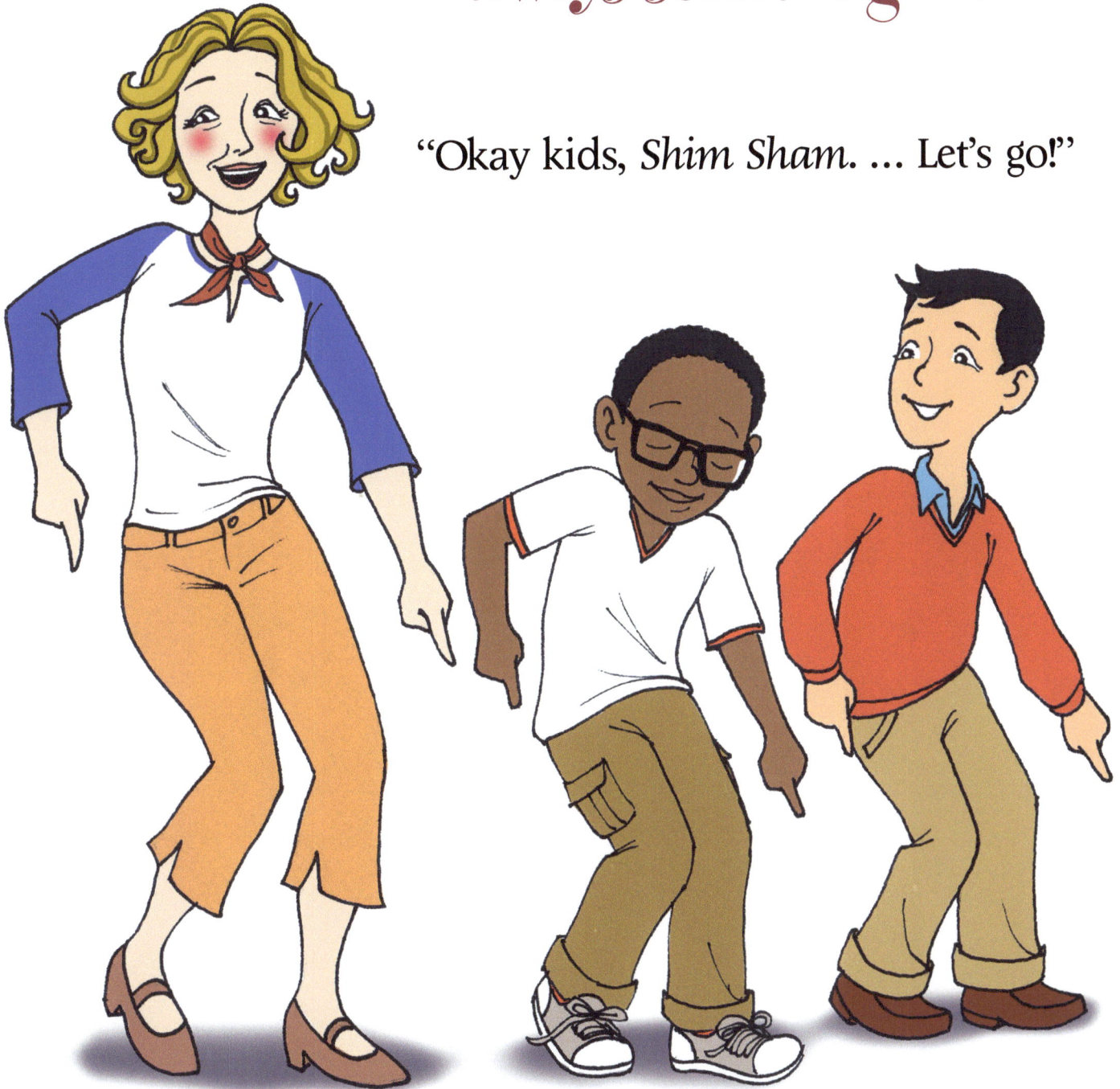

The Shim Sham Dance!

(Type these into your web browser)

It is recommended that teachers use Internet links to show children in their classes The *Shim Sham* dance.

Below are the links showing The *Shim Sham* created by the legendary Frankie Manning, choreographer/swing dancer.

http://www.youtube.com/watch?v=BpXOxBXUTOI&feature=related
*The London Swing Dance Society does the Shim Sham
on the streets of London*

http://www.youtube.com/watch?v=hubzPVG3f28

http://www.youtube.com/watch?v=tavoN2KI22k&feature=related

Beginners Shim Sham lesson

http://www.youtube.com/watch?v=s8D8m5YS_UI&feature=related

Note: Because of the dynamic nature of the Internet, any web addresses or links contained in this book may have changed since publication and no longer be valid.

artist
Dexter Santos

Dexter Santos has been drawing ever since he was 3 years old. His fascination with art started with the comic books he read and collected as well as the children's books that stimulated his imagination as a kid.

All throughout his elementary and high school years, Dexter participated in any event that had anything to do with drawing or painting and won for himself a handful of awards.

Continuing his passion for art as an adult, Dexter has seen his artwork manifested in art shows, on postcards, t-shirts, the Internet, the back of a bus, and even projected on a movie theater screen. This is the first time Dexter has illustrated for a children's book and he is excited and honored to tell the story of Auntie P and the wonderful lessons she imparts on young children.

Dexter has a BFA in Character Animation and Visual Effects from the Academy of Art University in San Francisco and currently resides in Santa Clara, California. Aside from being an artist, Dexter is also a nationally-renowned blues dance teacher and dancer. In his spare time, he likes to social dance, sing, play his ukulele, and go on afternoon motorcycle rides.

Find out more about Dexter's artwork at **dexterityink.com** and his dancing at **dextersantos.com**.

about the author
Patricia Kearney

Patricia Kearney, born in Brooklyn, New York and raised on Long Island, resides with her husband in New York City and in Lawrenceville, Pennsylvania. Her background experience includes producing in off-Broadway theatre and the music business.

Where's Grace? is her first children's book. Unlike Auntie P, who always travels by train, Ms. Kearney travels all over the world in trains, planes, boats, autos and also the occasional jaunting cart, especially when vacationing in the Republic of Ireland.

Ms. Kearney is married to playwright, director, composer and visual artist Ernest McCarty, Jr. of Chicago.

COMING SOON!

What's Sharing?

featuring Auntie P